MW00811455

The Mass
Explained to Children

THE MASS
Explained to Children

By
Maria Montessori

Foreword
by the Reverend
Matthew A. Delaney

Angelico Press

For information, address:
Angelico Press
4709 Briar Knoll Dr.
Kettering, OH 45429
info@angelicopress.com

978-1-62138-119-8 pb
978-1-62138-120-4 ebook

NIHIL OBSTAT: INNOCENTIUS APAP, S.TH.M., O.P.
CENSOR DEPUTATUS
IMPRIMATUR: ✝ JOSEPH BUTT,
VIC. GEN.
WESTMONASTERII, DIE XXA JUNII, MCMXXXII

Cover Design: Michael Schrauzer

CONTENTS

Foreword

ONE OF THE MOST significant trends in recent Church History has been the interest aroused in the Liturgy under the leadership of the Popes themselves. The Pope would have everybody share actively in the Liturgical life of the Church which expresses her worship of her Divine Master. And above all does he want every Christian to exercise his "holy priesthood" by actively participating in the supreme Liturgical act, the Mass.

This should come easily to the keen perceptions of children when they understand and value what the Mass really is. Doctor Montessori brings this home to them in her simple and accurate explanation which achieves the aim modern pedagogy would attain: it stimulates the interest of the child as an individual and brings him to think and to pray as a child does instinctively when he is really interested and not merely dragooned.

The children who use this book are indeed fortunate in thus having presented to them the fascinating action of the "Mystery of Faith."

MATTHEW A. DELANEY

March 25, 1933

Preface

THE RELIGIOUS EDUCATION of children took a great step forward when it was extended to the Liturgy, and an endeavor was made to teach the child how to follow ritual intelligently.

Since then the Missal for children's use and the method of teaching them how to take part in the Mass have become just as important factors in their religious education as the teaching of the catechism; whereas the latter was the only instruction they received up to the great reform of Pope Pius X.

Unfortunately, however, in putting this progress into practical effect the old-fashioned methods of education have been followed: adults still maintain towards children the same old misunderstanding of their character. They still think it necessary to interfere with them, continually and directly, to keep them from doing harm; and teachers imagine that the child is incapable of good without their exhortation or example. People had that idea, too, in the time of Christ; when children ran to the Divine Master they were pulled back by their elders, so that Our Lord had to rebuke them: "Suffer the little children to come unto Me." Moreover, this incident aroused Christ to a passing severity and He made it an opportunity for one of His divine revelations: "I say to you, unless you be converted, and become as little children, you shall not enter into the Kingdom of Heaven."

Our Lord perceived in children something that the adult did not perceive two thousand years ago and does not perceive today. Yet the Gospel says plainly that many mysteries shall be revealed to these little ones.

Christ's teaching about children touches the very core of their education; they have a different personality from ours, and spiritual impulses are alive in them which may be atrophied in the grown man.

We must always keep this fact in mind so that we may be prepared not only to offer children the noblest teaching, but to offer it in a worthy form.

We are bound to help children by teaching them what they need to know about religion, but we should not forget that the child can help us, too, by showing us the way to the Kingdom of Heaven. A great respect for the individuality of the child should be part of our deepest Christian thought; and putting this thought into practice should tend to the personal refinement of every religious teacher. There is much to be hoped from the spirituality of children. It is well to remember that during the Great War His Holiness Pope Benedict XV sent out a printed bull to be hung up in all the churches to be read by the faithful, and at the head of it he put these words: "I beg the dear and all-powerful children to hold up their hands for me at the altar."

THEREFORE, in this question of the liturgical education of children it is very important for us not only to teach them what they must know, but to lift ourselves to a much more sensitive frame of mind in order to be able to teach it.

It must be confessed that we adopt anything but the right attitude. It is a commonplace experience to listen in church to the rough and even abusive way children are admonished. Some lay masters lead files of children into church, rapping out orders to them like a corporal to a squad of new recruits: "Kneel down! No, not like that, all together!" Or one sees a teacher actually taking the children by the shoulders and placing them one by one in the benches, just as if she were packing fruit into baskets.

Another obvious mistake is to teach them *during* the Mass.

How often today one meets with those pious persons in church, who have taken on the work of conducting and teaching groups of children during Mass; and these children often include big boys, who at school are perhaps already learning algebra or the plays of Shakespeare. Even at the Consecration, during those moments of silence and recollection, one hears the voice of the zealous teacher raised—more often than not an unmusical and expressionless voice—droning out explanations, as though fulfilling a dry duty. The lesson over, a sharp "Sit up!" shoots all those young bodies upright again, and in those children—with the best intentions in the world—every spiritual impulse is thus stifled.

A somewhat similar error is found in most of the "Prayers at Mass" in books compiled especially for children. These books are overladen with instructions both in the text and in the pictures; so that they take up the child's whole attention and absorb all his energy. The reader of these little books must attend to the pictures, showing the position of the priest: now at the right of the altar, now turned towards it, now turned towards the people, and so forth; and the child must find the words of the text corresponding with those attitudes. In addition to all that, many of these little books contain pictures of the symbolical meaning of the various actions forming part of the rite; this represents the birth of Jesus, this His preaching, this His death and burial, and so on. Now we all know by experience how hard it is to follow Mass faithfully, even after years of practice, when we almost know the words by heart. How, therefore, can it be possible to follow it and learn it at the same time?

Is not the aim of the Mass to make us share in its mysteries, by yielding up the soul to God, in such recollection as is possible only by liberating our minds for a little while from all exterior distractions? This is the very reason why, in the first ages of Christianity, the catechumens were dismissed at the beginning of the Mass of the Faithful. One did not go to this part of Mass for instruction, which is an exterior thing; one went there to be united to Jesus Christ in the most intimate offering of the soul. Instruction in and sharing in the mysteries were seen to be two very different things, and were kept separate.

In actual fact the earliest division of the Mass into two parts was: the Mass of the Catechumens and the Mass of the Faithful. This should have great significance for us.

It is not necessary for the child to learn a great deal in order to follow Mass; but it is essential that he should be spiritually free if he is to follow it. In other words, teaching the Mass must not be mixed up with participation in it.

The Prayer Book for children should be like our Missal, that is, an actual copy of the liturgical text; and the instruction should be given in school or at home or, at any rate, some time other than during Holy Mass.

The majority of those striving today to improve the religious training of children have already agreed that the children's Missal should be a copy of the liturgical text.

But this text must be arranged in such a way as to make it easy for the child; and that where the new Missal still presents a problem. The text, although unaltered, can surely be adapted in the way it is presented, explained, and graduated, above all by calling into play the child's own activity; because it is proved by now that children are at their best when actively co-operating.

However, this is not the place for me to explain what a children's Missal should be.

It is a very wide subject, and I am treating it in another book written especially on the Children's Mass.

Preface for Children

"That which was from the beginning,
Which we have heard,
Which we have seen with our eyes,
Which we have looked upon,
And our hands have handled…
We declare unto you,
That you also may have fellowship with us,
And our fellowship may be with the Father,
And with His Son Jesus Christ."

Thus spoke John, the disciple whom Jesus loved.

The Last Supper

Jesus said to Peter and John:

GO, AND PREPARE FOR US THE PASCH, THAT WE MAY
EAT.
YOU WILL FIND A LARGE DINING-ROOM, FURNISHED;
AND THERE PREPARE.

And they prepared the table.
And when the hour was come, He sat down, and the
Twelve Apostles with Him.
And He said to them:

WITH DESIRE I HAVE DESIRED TO EAT THIS PASCH WITH
YOU, BEFORE I SUFFER. FOR I SAY TO YOU THAT FROM
THIS TIME I WILL NOT EAT IT TILL IT BE FULFILLED IN
THE KINGDOM OF GOD.

And having taken the chalice, He gave thanks, and said:

TAKE, AND DIVIDE IT AMONG YOU: FOR I SAY TO YOU
THAT I WILL DRINK NO MORE OF THE FRUIT OF THE
VINE TILL THE KINGDOM OF GOD COME... THIS IS THE
CHALICE OF MY BLOOD WHICH SHALL BE SHED FOR YOU
AND FOR MANY UNTO THE REMISSION OF SINS.

And taking bread He gave thanks, and brake; and gave to them, saying:

THIS IS MY BODY, WHICH IS GIVEN FOR YOU. DO THIS FOR A COMMEMORATION OF ME.

I

The Meaning of the Mass

OUR LORD JESUS CHRIST said the first Mass at the Last Supper. Ever since then, His disciples have gone on looking for a large furnished room where they may prepare the table for Him.

You can see this for yourself when you go to Mass. The large furnished dining-room is the church, and the altar there is the table, prepared with its white cloths. A precious chalice stands on it for holding the wine and water, and also a plate containing a round piece of bread. You will see a man, too, standing by the prepared table; he is the priest who represents Christ. He repeats the very words which Christ said to the Apostles around Him: "Take ye and eat, for this is My Body"; and in the same way, taking the chalice, he repeats: "This is the Chalice of My Blood . . . which shall be shed for the remission of sins."

And the faithful who are pure in heart lovingly and devoutly approach the table to receive the Sacred Host, just as the Apostles received it at the Last Supper from the hands of Christ: because He said: "I am the living bread, which came down from heaven. If any man eat of this bread, he shall live for ever: and the bread that I will give is My flesh for the life of the world."

THE MYSTERY

HOLY MASS, however, is not merely a commemoration. It may *look* no more than that to people who have not penetrated its mysteries. They may think it a rite carried out in memory of the dead Christ since, as a living Man, He has gone from this earth. Here then, they think, is His memorial service: there is the image of Jesus Crucified, an unchanging symbol in the center of the table, with lighted candles burning around it. The whole thing is exactly like a pious remembrance of His death.

But the Mass is by no means such a simple matter.

We do not go to it merely to commemorate the Passion of Christ as an act of piety, which we always owe Him.

Here there is no real death.

What seems death is Life.

There is a deep mystery hidden in the Mass, a supernatural, astounding fact, the greatest wonder of all: Jesus, at a certain moment, comes down alive on the altar. He is invisible, but He is truly present, because the bread is changed into His Body, and the wine into His Blood; so that Christ is there, Body, Blood, Soul, and Divinity, and He comes for us…

Therefore, when we go to Mass, we do not go there only to commemorate Jesus; we go to find Him, to receive Him. He is present there, He lives, and He will never leave us.

This is our comfort, our hope, the greatest part of our Faith: the Mystery of the Mass.

We have not been left orphans alone in the world. When Christ ascended into Heaven, He did not abandon us. He promised not to: "I WILL NOT LEAVE YOU ORPHANS." So, every time we come from Holy Mass, we can cry out like Magdalen, rejoicing: "He is alive! I have spoken to Him."

The mystery of the Mass can be summed up in one single fact.

When the priest, celebrating at the altar, in commemoration of Jesus, speaks certain words, the same as those spoken by Him at the Last Supper, the Living Christ truly descends on the altar, to give Himself to men and to live in their hearts.

He comes in that solemn moment called the Consecration, when all the faithful kneel with their eyes intent on the outward sign of the Great Mystery.

The Host that is raised up is the Body of the Living Christ.

The Chalice that is lifted up contains His Blood.

This Mystery has sometimes been accompanied by visible miracles, seen not only by holy persons, who were assisting at Mass with great faith; but even by people of little fervor, or by absolute unbelievers.

Once a holy hermit saw the Child Jesus in the Host, and the vision at the Elevation radiated a marvelous light. Once, too, it happened that a priest accidentally upset the chalice, in which the wine was already consecrated, and spilled it on the altar cloth. The wine, which was white, left red stains like blood, and although the cloth was washed and washed over again, the stains could not be removed.

The story is also told of Wittikind, the fierce King of the Saxons, that he was converted to Christianity because he saw in the Host at the Elevation the face of a little boy smiling at him.

These miracles, and others like them, have happened in every part of the world.

But the real wonder is worked sacramentally by Christ's coming into the hearts of Christians. The greatest wonder of all is what takes place at every Mass: the real presence of Jesus, hidden from our eyes, but truly present to our faith.

Jesus remains, thus hidden under the appearance of the Sacrament, which is kept in the locked Tabernacle. So every time a Catholic enters the church, he bows down devoutly before Him.

The church is a holy place because of this Real Presence of Jesus.

But it is only in the Mass and at no other time that He comes down to us under the appearance of bread and wine, just as so many centuries ago He became Man in the most pure womb of the Blessed Virgin Mary.

THE CHURCH

YOU CAN well imagine how men would flock around such a mystery, such a stupendous miracle as this.

Since the night of the Last Supper, followed by the Passion and Resurrection of Christ, and by the descent of the Holy Ghost, Christians have gathered closely together in the Church.

But Christians are not united in the Catholic Church merely in memory of the Messiah foretold by the prophets, the Master and Savior of men, who suffered and died for love of those who had sinned so much against Him. Catholics are not merely *believers* in a divine teaching, such as Christ gave to men when He lived among them and taught them as a Teacher.

They are united in this mystery of the Living Christ's continuous return to the world, that they may receive Him and live in Him.

In a sense we Catholics live a miraculous life in the Church, because, as we believe, we become one thing with Christ.

It is from Him we must get the strength to live His doctrines. Man can learn the very noblest teaching, but he needs the grace of God if he is to practice it. Indeed, he must lose himself in God, because it is Christ in us who can do all things.

So it is to nothing less than this that the Catholic aspires: "*I live, now not I: but Christ liveth in me.*"

THE HISTORY OF THE MASS

AGAIN we say, it is easy to imagine what a strong religious life developed around this mystery. It inspired the marvelous deeds of the first Christians and the courage of the martyrs.

Even little children shared in the miraculous strength infused by the living Christ: the martyr, Pancras, was only a child; Tarcisius was a little altar-boy who died to defend the Blessed Sacrament; and there were many other children like that.

But remember, it is not enough just to hear the promises of Our Lord in order to enter into the Kingdom of Christ and win eternal life. No, He must really live in our hearts.

The history of the Church is also the history of the Mass.

In the early ages of Christianity, when the Church was persecuted, Christians used to meet in the Catacombs (underground passages and cellars in Rome) to celebrate Mass there. Or sometimes they would hide in the house of some rich Christian, as in the houses of Saints Bibiana and Pudentiana in Rome. They would seek there a place suitable for the mystical banquet, and then they would prepare the table just as in the Last Supper.

Or, if there did not happen to be a rich Christian among them who could lend them a fine house, they might meet in a humble cabin belonging to poor people, who perhaps had only one room, where their kitchen utensils hung on the old blackened walls.

But poverty did not matter. The only thing that mattered was faith. So there, too, the cloth was spread on a little table, and all those Christians, who were ready to die for Christ, knelt around it with rapt gaze and expectant hearts, waiting for the Living Lord who would descend upon earth for them. And often, indeed, for those first Christians the Mass was a Last Supper too, because on going out from it, the glorious death of martyrdom awaited them.

Like everything else that begins with a great reality, the way of celebrating Mass went on perfecting itself through the centuries, becoming gradually the wonderful rite it is today.

Once upon a time the Mass was longer than it is now. When Christians emerged from the age of persecution, their joy was so great in proclaiming aloud the glory of the Lord and their eagerness to honor Him so intense that they spent half the day gathered around the great Mystery. In Rome they used to have long processions, in which the Pope walked barefoot and all the Christians sang hymns; and then they would all go in together to one of the great churches to hear Mass.

But not all were allowed to be present during Mass, as we are today, because not all were baptized Christians.

CATECHUMENS AND FAITHFUL

THE CATECHUMENS (those who were learning to be Christians but were not yet baptized) were allowed to be present only at the beginning of Mass, to hear the Sacred Scriptures, especially the Gospel, read aloud, since that was a general instruction for all Christians.

This first part was like a sort of introduction to the real mysteries of the Mass. The people joined with the priests and bishops in the singing of hymns, making the responses to the psalms, and also listening to the reading and explanation of the Gospels.

But when the actual Mass was to begin, the Catechumens were dismissed with the words "Dominus Vobiscum," which mean "God be with you." These words were a way of taking leave, just as we use the word "Good-bye" today.

The priest said "Good-bye" to them, and off they went.

Then the Faithful came forward.

They did not come with empty hands, but rather brought offerings. Usually they brought what was needed for the Mass: bread of unleavened flour, pure wine of the grape, money for the Church and for the ceremony, and also charitable offerings for poor Christians.

So there was a great bustle, often with a lot of noise. Alms were asked for the poor; the names of those who could not come to the Mass but wished to be prayed for were read out, and the greater part of those present sang the special hymns and psalms of the day.

At last the actual Mass began with the offering up to God of the bread and wine to be consecrated, and of the hearts of all the faithful. This was a time of silence and of devout recollection.

THE SACRED RITE represents the Passion of Christ, the offering up of Jesus, who gave Himself a Victim for the salvation of men. The Church has commanded special words and actions to be used, in order to present the drama of Jesus Christ with scrupulous fidelity.

Everything is sacred in the rite of Holy Mass. Every movement of the priest, every object he touches, every tone of his voice, is determined for him: and the faithful can follow the Mass in its mystical meaning and in its every detail. But the aim of the faithful is to *share* in the Mass: to await the coming of Christ and to communicate with the Living Jesus.

THE COMMUNION OF SAINTS

IT IS BEAUTIFUL to think what activity there must be in Heaven about the offering of the Mass. The pure spirits see clearly what is such a mystery to us; first of all, the most Blessed Virgin Mary sees, and with her all the Angels and Saints of Paradise.

They understand what infinite love leads Christ continually to us; and rejoicing Angels form His crown and escort. They gaze upon the children present at Mass, and rejoice in the privilege that is theirs.

Then all the Saints, and especially the martyrs who shed their blood like Christ, plead around the altar. To gladden us and to help us, they offer all their merits to our souls; they are in communion with us. Yes, the merits which they acquired while they were living on the earth can be used by us as if they were ours. This is a most precious spiritual gift permitted by God, and is the heart of the doctrine of the Communion of Saints.

Let us never forget it.

We know they want to help us. And when we most feel our meanness and the need of God's mercy, let us invoke our Saints and holy Patrons:

"I beseech blessed Mary, ever a Virgin, blessed Michael the Archangel, blessed John the Baptist, the holy Apostles

Peter and Paul, and all the Saints to pray to the Lord our God for me."

THE MASS BELLS

THE EARLY HOURS of the morning are the most beautiful and the holiest hours of the day. From the rising of the sun, the different bells begin to chime in turn, telling the time of Holy Mass and calling the faithful to rise quickly from their beds to come and meet Our Lord.

When you hear these bells, think of Abraham. When God called him, he was ready to obey even to the sacrifice of his dear and only son.

And you are not asked to make a sacrifice, like Abraham. On the contrary, you are called to receive infinite grace.

Come then! Come!

Beautiful holy hours of the morning, when Mass is being offered up all over the world!

THE SPIRITUAL ATMOSPHERE

MASS IS OFFERED in the morning, because those who wish to receive Our Lord in Holy Communion, both priests and people, must be fasting from the midnight before.

The first rays of sunrise tell us that the Bread of angels is ready for us; and the prayer which Jesus Himself taught us has become the daily invocation on our lips: *"Give us this day our daily bread."*

Think for a moment that the earth is round and that the sun never leaves it. When it is midday here, it is midnight on the opposite side of the earth, and all the people there are sound asleep. But there, too, the day begins to dawn, and when it is late afternoon with us, the sun is rising there, and those far-away bells begin to ring out from the churches, calling the faithful who live at the other end of the world.

If you study the map well, you can easily see that it is morning in some part of the world at every hour of the day. You can even find out in what countries Christians are expecting Christ each hour of the twenty-four.

Our Lord "never ceases to come."

Since the death of Christ, the earth is compassed about with the spirits of angels and saints. And that spiritual atmosphere of immense goodness helps men's souls to live; just as the material atmosphere of air helps their bodies to live.

THE CALL

EVERY CHILD can make this little meditation each morning:

"Is it true that Jesus has come for me? Specially for me?

Yes, it is true: He has called me.

It is an absolute fact.

Each one of us has been called.

Christ said to us, with outstretched arms:

'Come unto Me!

Suffer the little children to come unto Me.

Come unto Me all ye who labor and are burdened, and I will refresh you.

Come unto Me all ye who are afflicted, and I will console you.

In Me is peace.'"

II

What is Necessary for the Mass

PREPARING THE TABLE

THE ALTAR represents a table which recalls the Last Supper. But the word "altar" does not mean "table"; it means a "high thing," from the Latin *altus,* high. And in practice we know an altar from a table by its height, as an altar is always raised above the ground on steps.

The most simple kind of altar is an oblong, rectangular slab, supported by four little columns—the legs of the table. But also, in the past, a stone altar supported by only one column in the center, like a garden table, was sometimes used.

Another kind of altar is similar in shape to a tomb. This arose long ago from the fact that, when they could not use a building above ground for the celebration of Mass, the first Christians often went underground and used the tombs of the martyrs in the Catacombs as altars. Indeed many of the altars still in use in the great churches of Europe are tombs, made of stone or precious marble, in which are preserved the bodies of saints.

The flat top of the altar should be a stone slab with five crosses engraved on it; one in the center and one at each of the four corners, to represent the five wounds of Christ. If there is no such stone altar available, as often happens in new or poor parishes, or when Mass is said in the open air, or in private houses, it is sufficient to put a much smaller stone, called the altar-stone, on any raised structure, even on an ordinary piece of furniture, to make an altar.

This altar-stone is a square slab. It may be as small as a large tile, although it is often made somewhat larger when it is to be used permanently in a church having only a wooden altar. On its upper surface are engraved five crosses, exactly as they are on a larger, fixed altar. In the altar-stone, as indeed in all altars where Mass is celebrated, is embedded a small leaden box, about the size of an ordinary match box, which contains the relics of at least one sainted martyr. These relics must be obtained from Rome, where an account is kept of all those sent out through the whole world to be embedded in the thousands of altars where Mass is celebrated.

Rome is the very garden of the saints. In the Coliseum there, and in the ancient churches built out of the noble palaces of Roman converts, the bodies of all those who died for the Faith were preserved with honor, so that the relics of martyrs abound there like blades of grass in a field. All this reminds us of the multitude of heroes who fell in the bloody battle for Christianity, to win the reign of peace in the whole world. The martyrs gave their blood without shedding that of their fellow men, because they offered themselves for death, forgiving their enemies and promising them the Kingdom of Heaven.

So the saints, the great soldiers of Christianity, are put there on the altar like sentinels at the gate of the Eternal King, to keep watch throughout the centuries.

During Mass the bread and wine—which are to be changed into the Living Christ—stand on the altar-stone, near the relics of some martyr saint, and after the Consecration, the Sacred Species are placed on the same spot.

The moment the priest goes up the altar steps, he kisses this stone as a salute to the venerable sentinels, and he says:

"Through the merits of Thy saints whose relics lie here, deign to forgive me all my sins, O Lord!"

THE ALTAR STEPS

THE HOLY TABLE is on a higher level, and there are steps leading up to it.

These steps are usually three in number, and are a symbol of the three theological virtues which lead us to God: faith, hope, and charity. The steps are really part of the altar itself, and the Mass begins at the foot of them.

Very often, in the big churches and basilicas, you will see altars built high up, so that one has to climb a series of steps on different levels to reach the high altar. All these stairs are "accessories of honor," but they do not belong to the altar itself. However high up this may be placed, it will still have its own three steps, before which the priest must stop when he begins to celebrate Mass.

THE THREE ALTAR-CLOTHS

THE ALTAR is covered with three white cloths of real linen. At one time all these cloths were very long, often reaching to the ground.

But today the altar-cloths must be arranged as follows: two small ones which cover only the top of the altar; and another very much longer one, but of the same width, which is placed over the others and falls down at each side, right and left. This latter is the real altar-cloth.

THE THREE ORNAMENTS

THREE THINGS must be placed on every altar: a Crucifix, which is put in the center and a little to the back, and at least two candles of pure beeswax, one at each side. The altar Crucifix has a little support so that it stands upright, and of course the two candles are placed in candlesticks.

Even if these ornaments are of the very plainest kind, they serve the purpose. The Crucifix is a loving, insistent reminder that Jesus was taken and killed on the Cross after the Last Supper. The candles of pure wax, which are lighted and burn for the whole of Mass, are to remind us that Christ suffered to illuminate mankind with His light of love, pardon, and peace.

Of course these three ornaments are often richly ornamented as an offering of love to Christ.

ADDITIONAL ORNAMENTS OF LOVE

You will sometimes see many other ornaments above or beside the altar, such as candles, little lamps, banners, statues of gold and silver, and vases of lovely fresh flowers. All these things are accessories; but they are not superfluous, because nothing is ever superfluous that is offered out of love of Christ.

However, you must distinguish carefully between the "ornaments of the rite," which *must* be there, and the "accessories" which can be very varied. If there are no accessories whatever, it makes no difference to the rite.

PREPARING THE ALTAR FOR MASS

Now LET US see what is wanted to prepare the altar for Mass. Even a child can do all that is necessary; as a matter of fact, it is very often little boys who prepare the altar for Mass and serve it.

The Light.—When Mass is about to begin, the candles are lighted by means of a taper fastened on to a long stick. The stick has usually a little cone on it, too, for putting out the lights when the Mass is over.

The Book.—At the right of the altar (that is, the right side to those who are looking at it) there is placed a book-rest, or a cushion, on which is laid a big book: the *Missal.* The boy is allowed to bring the holy book and put it in its place. He puts it down, closed, on the support. The priest opens it at the proper place before beginning the celebration of the Mass.

The Water and Wine.—Two other things which must be prepared immediately before Mass begins are the water and wine. These are prepared in clean cruets in a little dish, which are put on a table near the altar, usually at the right side of it, or perhaps on a little shelf attached to the wall for that purpose.

The Towel.—A small white towel, well ironed and neatly folded, is placed beside the cruets; this is used by the priest for drying his fingers. The Mass server holds it on his arm and offers it to the celebrant at the right time. It is called the finger-towel, or mundatory.

The Bell.—Finally, there is one other thing necessary, and that is a bell, which is placed on the steps within reach of the boy serving Mass.

And now the acolyte, or the boy who is serving the Mass, has done everything necessary to prepare the altar for the arrival of the officiating priest.

THE SACRED VESSELS

THE CHALICE and paten used for the celebration of Mass are so sacred that no layman ordinarily touches them.

They come into direct contact with the Body and Blood of Christ in the Mass, and no hand that is not consecrated for the priesthood ever comes in contact with them. Therefore the priest himself must carry them.

The priest, vested to say Mass, carries in his hand the mysterious wrapping, of which you can see only the outer covering.

That covering is nearly always made of silk and is the same color as the priest's vestment. This is not merely to have everything nicely matching, but because not only the ornaments, but even the very colors used (the liturgical colors) are determined by the rubric or regulation for every day in the year.

The first thing the priest does is to go up and rest this mysterious burden on the altar; he lays it down gently, settling the folds of the little cover carefully so as to have everything perfect. He places it exactly over the altar-stone.

When he has done this, the priest goes over to the book and opens it at the right page for the Mass of that day.

Remember, the Mass has not begun: what the priest is

doing now is making the final preparations and nothing else.

When he has done this, he descends the steps.

The Mass begins at the foot of the three steps.

WHAT THE PRIEST CARRIES

Now LET US see what is under that cover which the priest has placed on the altar.

Resting on the top of it is a hard, square folder: it is a kind of flat purse covered with colored silk and usually ornamented by a cross. This is called the *Burse*.

It contains a square of white linen, ironed in such a way that it is perfectly smooth and flat. It is folded in a very special way: one fold from the side near you, one fold from the top, then one fold from each side so that, when it is spread out, there are nine squares in it.

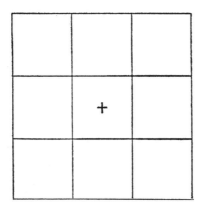

This piece of white linen is called the *Corporal* (from *corpus,* Latin for "body"). It has the great honor of touching the Body of Christ, because the priest lays the Sacred Host upon it.

The Chalice also rests on the unfolded Corporal, so that if a drop of the Blood of Christ should spill, it would fall on the Corporal.

You can understand now why the Corporal is a most sacred cloth.

No one is allowed to wash it except a priest, deacon, or subdeacon. Only after this first washing are lay people allowed to touch it to finish the laundering and iron it in the way described above.

A plain linen cloth is used for a Corporal. It is always kept and carried about in the Burse, which is often very richly embroidered because it is used to cover such a sacred thing.

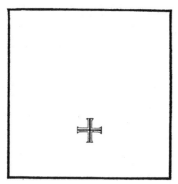

Now let us take away the square silk cloak that covers everything underneath the Burse. It is made of heavy material, usually brocade with a silk lining, and is called the *Veil.*

Now we have discovered what stands under the Veil.

A *Chalice* and a *Plate*: the things used long ago at the Supper of Christ have become the Sacred Vessels of the Eucharistic Table.

In the plate (called the *Paten*) there is a large white Host, which is to be consecrated during Mass. But the Chalice is empty.

Both Chalice and Paten are made of precious metal, even in the very poorest churches. They cannot be made of anything but silver or gold, however plain and simple. An inferior metal is not allowed.

But one rarely finds them plain and simple: love and devotion usually lead the faithful to ornament the sacred vessels and to enrich them with precious stones, making them into great treasures. The very finest engraving, the most beautiful and the rarest gems have been lavished on those two vessels throughout all the history of Christianity.

They are arranged under the Veil in a special way. The Chalice stands on the altar. A linen cloth, folded three times lengthwise, is placed across the cup of the Chalice and hangs down at each side. On this cloth rests the Paten containing the Host, and covering the Paten is another piece of linen about the same size as it.

The linen cloth placed across the Chalice is called the *Purificator* and is almost part of it, because it is used to clean the inside of the Chalice and therefore to remove the last traces of the consecrated wine which may be left after the ablutions. Therefore, this cloth also is very sacred and cannot be touched by any hands save those of the priest.

The Chalice from which the priest drinks the consecrated wine is never washed until it has been wiped well and cleaned with the Purificator. No one can do that but the priest who has said the Mass, and he does it before he puts the Sacred Vessels back under the Veil.

Lastly, there is that other little piece of linen, starched quite stiff, and used as a cover. It first of all covers the Paten under the Veil; afterwards the priest uses it several times during Mass to cover the Chalice. This little piece of linen is called the *Pall*.

THE BREAD AND WINE

THE BREAD AND WINE of the Eucharistic table are the materials to be changed into the Body and Blood of Christ. After the consecration, what is present visibly is called the Species.

From a sense of devotion, Christians have always prepared these materials with special care, to mark their difference from what is used for the ordinary food of men. Their first tendency was to make them scrupulously from the very purest things. They have done this since the very earliest ages, even when they put on the altar the big, ordinary sort of loaf of bread that everyone used, but marked with a cross or with a fish, which was the symbol of Christ for the early Christians. The first Eucharistic breads were made of pure wheat, without any mixing, ground into flour, kneaded with pure water and then baked at the fire. Afterwards, instead of a loaf, wafers were used, but they were made in the same way and stamped with various sacred symbols. The Host used by the priest nowadays is large and ornamented with such symbols; while the hosts, or particles (little portions), given to the faithful in Holy Communion, are much smaller and often have nothing stamped on them.

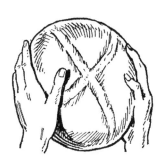

Then the wine is made of pure grape-juice, without any mixture, except that when the pure wine is in the Chalice, the priest adds a little water. This action recalls an incident in the Passion, when the soldier pierced the side of Christ and blood and water issued.

That is why such ordinary things as the wheat and the grape have such tremendous importance for us Christians. They become a mysterious food, which only we can understand. Just as our soul lives in the world by means of the flesh of our bodies, so God remains among us under the Species which come from the wheat and the grape. After the consecration the *latens deitas*, the Hidden Godhead, lies under those humble appearances.

The cultivation of the plants destined for such a noble use inspires Christians with great devotion; even the clods of earth which feed these plants have something sacred for us which sets them apart. The fields of wheat and the vines that are to give the bread and wine for the Eucharist cannot be confused with the vast fields of corn and the rich vineyards which man cultivates for himself by the sweat of his brow.

The former are almost "particles" of earth, small plots, because very little wheat and only a very small vine are sufficient to provide the materials for the Eucharist.

This is the reason why the plan was formed in Italy some years ago of turning over to the children the cultivation of such plots. It had already been done in a school in Barcelona. Two fields were set apart for the purpose, side by side, one for the wheat and the other for the vine. These fields were surrounded with flowering plants which would give flowers in every season, especially an abundance of roses.

The harvesting of the wheat and the vintage of the wine

were then made great country festivals, carried out with the most beautiful ceremonies.

The idea that children are the most suitable for cultivating the Eucharistic fields, and for taking part in the making of the hosts and the wine, is only the latest of many such devout ideas which Christians have had from the very earliest times.

At one time it was the most illustrious and powerful personages in the kingdom, such as queens and princes, who reserved this honor for themselves; one old writer says:

". . . I saw with my own eyes Candida, the wife of Trajan, General-in-Command of the armies of Valerius, spend the whole night in grinding the wheat and making with her own hands the bread of oblation. . . ."

The holy Queen Radegonde used to make the Eucharistic bread and bake it during Lent.

Towards the end of the ninth century, a cardinal recommended deacons, chosen to make the altar-breads, to vest themselves in their blessed habits for this work and to sing psalms while they were doing it.

It is said that in some parts of France it used to be the custom to choose the wheat grain by grain; and the very holiest person in the district was chosen to take it to the mill, dressed in white, as in a solemn ceremony.

Even a reverence for the sods of earth is related in ancient history. People used to leave as heritage little plots of ground that they loved, dedicating them to the cultivation of the wheat that would supply "the pure, holy, and stainless Host."

It is faith that makes people do these things: those who are imbued with faith show a great delicacy of love in all their actions.

THE PRIEST

So YOU SEE that the earth gives nourishment to the wheat and the vine.

The wheat and the vine grow and make the material substance of the bread and wine.

The Christian man makes Eucharistic bread out of the wheat, and pure wine out of the clusters of grapes.

But there is only one sort of man with hands sacred and pure enough to offer the bread and wine. There is only one sort of man who can raise his eyes to Heaven, with power to speak the words which Christ commanded to be spoken if He was to descend among us, according to His promise; one sort of man only, and that is a priest.

He is the link between God and man; the instrument for putting earth in touch with Heaven.

So there are not only sacred things, but sacred people too.

Although, in a sense, his office is slight—almost like that of a hand switching on the electricity at night and brilliantly lighting up a room—still, it is he alone who can do it; it is to him we owe that final touch which permits us thus to communicate with God.

It is he who can say: "Vouchsafe, Almighty God, that what is being done by means of Thy humble minister, may be accomplished by Thy power."

It is the priest's hands only that may touch the Sacred Species and distribute them to us as the spiritual food instituted by Christ.

> *For My Flesh is meat indeed:*
> *And My Blood is drink indeed.*
> *He that eateth My Flesh,*
> *And drinketh My Blood,*
> *Abideth in Me,*
> *And I in him.*

Let us look at the priest with reverence, let us love him gratefully, let us never forget him in our prayers, because he has given up his life to us.

He, too, was once a child just like you, and he used to play away thoughtlessly at his games, but his heart was filled with a great love for Christ.

Then one day he "heard the call" and knew what it meant. He was not a priest then, and perhaps did not even know he would become one.

But when he felt himself called, he made the same answer that Christ made to the Eternal Father: "Thy will be done."

If it were only because of that call, we should revere him.

35

But he is greater still because he resolved to answer it and become virtuous in his heart. He resolved to be faithful to the end; and he was made a priest for all eternity.

It is with him that Jesus Christ, through the Church, His Spouse, concluded a divine pact, saying in effect:

"When you repeat at the Holy Altar the words which I spoke to the Apostles when consecrating and offering the bread and wine, I WILL COME."

Look at him well: he is the very personification of obedience. He will not say one word different from what he has been commanded to say; every movement he makes has been determined for him. His vestments and their colors have all been prescribed for him.

He can say: "It is not I who live, but Christ, whom I represent."

THE SACRED VESTMENTS

THE PRIEST who is getting ready to say Mass vests himself according to the prescriptions of the rite.

Like a great court dignitary, who must appear before the king, he dresses according to the very strictest etiquette.

Whether they are very rich or quite plain, the sacred vestments should always be dignified. The different parts of the complete dress are always the same, because they are ordered by the rubric.

Now here, just as in the case of the ornaments used on the altar at Mass, you must distinguish between what is absolutely indispensable and what may be added by way of accessories.

No one has a better right to wear rich garments than the priest celebrating Mass, and, as a matter of fact, the sacred vestments are sometimes made of the most magnificent materials, such as silk and gold damask, and covered with embroidery and gems. Fabrics of the most extraordinary beauty are worked by loving hands in the silence of cloisters to clothe the priest of God.

You must now learn the names of the different vestments. They are put on over the usual clothes. The priest or the monk does not take off his ordinary habit, but he puts on the vestments over it. While they are saying Mass, the priest and monk have a special dignity *over and above* what they already possess as men, and therefore they put on over their ordinary clothes the vestments which represent that additional dignity.

You see, the man is less than the priest. Under the magnificent priestly vestments is the man, who is just the servant of God. This man must be full of reverence for the Mass which he is preparing to say, and while he is vesting, he must be recollected and pray. He says a special prayer with every vestment he puts on, and he does this slowly and devoutly.

The vestments which the priest wears for celebrating Mass are made like the clothes which even lay people wore once upon a time. But the priest's vestments have always remained unchanged, except in shape, whereas lay people change theirs continually according to the fashion of the day, so that now the sacred vestments are absolutely unlike any others.

In addition, on account of their high purpose, the sacred vestments came little by little to have a symbolical meaning, as though they were an armor of defense. The priest represents the soldier of Christ who arms himself and goes to the combat, to overcome evil by good and make the Kingdom of Christ triumphant in the world.

The sacred vestments are of two kinds: linen vestments and outer vestments. The linen vestments are:

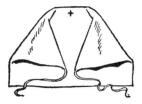

I. The Amice.—This is a white linen cloth which in ancient times served to cover the head, and is now worn around the neck and over the shoulders. The word "amice" comes from the Latin and means a covering. It is like a little hood. In its mystical meaning, it is the *helmet of salvation,* almost like those steel helmets which soldiers put on to protect their heads.

II. The Alb.—This is a very wide tunic made of linen which covers the whole body down to the feet, with big sleeves reaching down to the wrists. All white, it represents the innocence which clothes the Christian soul through the merits of Christ.

III. The Girdle.—This is a long white cord tied around the waist, to draw in the wide tunic. It is the symbol of chastity.

The vestments which are not of linen are all made of the same material, in a set to match. They are:

I. The Maniple.—This is a band which is worn round the left arm. It is a symbol of Our Lord's Passion.

II. The Stole.—This is another band like the Maniple, but longer, and it is worn around the neck and crossed on the breast. The stole is the symbol of immortality.

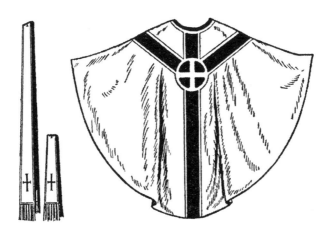

III. The Chasuble.—This is a large outer vestment which, in olden times, fell down in stately folds, and then was reduced by degrees to that stiff covering which you often see today. This vestment represents the yoke of Christ, the mild yoke of His law of love, which is, however, marked by the necessity for sacrifice: the Cross.

THE LITURGICAL COLORS

THE DIFFERENT COLORS of the Chasuble (and, therefore, of all the vestments and things of the same material which the priest wears or uses during the celebration of Mass) are ordered by the Church for the different seasons and days of the year, and are called the liturgical colors.

There is a special color for each festive season, and for the feast-days of the saints celebrated in the daily Mass. But the number of colors is limited. They are:

Red, the color of the martyrs; *white,* the color of holiness; red is also the color for Pentecost and white is the color for Christmas. When the season is one of sadness or penance, as in Lent or during Holy Week, then the color is *violet.* It is *black* if the Mass is offered up for a departed soul. On days when nothing special is to be commemorated the color *green* is used. No other colors but those five are normally allowed at the altar, except gold and silver.

THAT COMPLETES the description of the sacred vestments used in the celebration of Mass.

When Benediction is given, as it sometimes is after a High Mass, you will see the priest put on an additional cloak over certain of the vestments described above. This cloak is usually a gorgeous mantle like those a king wears when he sits on his throne.

But this mantle—the *Cope*—is not really for the officiating priest: it is really meant to clothe Christ reigning in the Sacrament. Over it again the priest wears the *Humeral Veil* which is wrapped over his shoulders and round his hands.

The priest becomes very small and is almost hidden beneath those wrappings; he only serves to support them. The King is there in that Sacred Host, turning towards His faithful people, and the priest, as God's minister, gives them his blessing.

III

Introduction to the Mass

THE DIVINE THEATRE

THE MASS is a mystery. It is not possible for us to understand the infinite goodness God shows us in the great mystery of transubstantiation.

But there is nothing secret about it. Everyone, even the smallest child, may hear or read every word of it and see every action.

The method prescribed by the Church for celebrating Mass makes it into a wonderful drama, as in some heavenly theatre.

This is because Christians naturally gave outward expression to their great faith. In commemorating the life of the Savior and in their desire of God, they would meet together to pray, sing, and worship. They collected the most beautiful words and the noblest actions that sincere devotion could inspire. That is why the Mass is a representative action and became fixed in consecutive, unified parts, like the acts and scenes in a great drama, the drama of Redemption.

But the priest is not the only actor; no, the Mass is above all the action of Christendom, of the Church. The Church is not made up of priests only, but of all Catholics, and so the people have their part in the Mass.

The congregation at Mass do not merely look on; they are actors in the drama. When the priest speaks, the people answer him; when he prays, the people unit themselves with him. The feelings of love, expectation and gratitude expressed by the priest officiating at the altar are re-echoed in the hearts of the people. They all become one thing together, one single voice, lifted up to Heaven.

THE PARTS OF THE MASS

THE WHOLE MASS is divided into two parts:

The Mass of the Catechumens (or Mass of Instruction), and the Mass of the Faithful.

The first part culminates in the *reading of the Gospel*: that is, in the Word of God. Then the priest may add to this reading a sermon of his own, explaining the Gospel and so instructing the people.

This first part commemorates the Living Jesus, from the time of His birth, during His tender childhood, and ends by showing Him preaching to the crowds in Palestine.

The second part culminates in the *Consecration* and in the *Elevation of the Host and Chalice*—the Body and the Blood of Christ.

It commemorates the Passion of Christ and the great sacrifice made by God for the salvation of men.

In this way the whole Mass recalls the whole life of Christ.

And, indeed, before Christ offered Himself as a sacrifice on the Cross, He instructed men, teaching them by word the doctrines of His Heavenly Father.

The principal part of the Mass is the second, because it recalls the redemption of all mankind which was brought about by the sacrifice offered by Christ.

The Mass of the Faithful is, in its turn, divided into three parts. The first part is the offering of the bread and wine to be consecrated, together with the offering up of all hearts to God.

The second part is the Consecration, in which God made man is really present and offered.

The third part is the Mass of peace, in which men, through Holy Communion, become united with God.

THE REPRESENTATIVE OBJECTS

THE REPRESENTATIVE OBJECTS of the two main parts of the Mass are:

In the Mass of the Catechumens: the Book.

In the Mass of the Faithful: the Host and the Chalice.

To these may be added: in the Mass of the Catechumens, the pulpit for preaching, where the speaker can be seen and from which his voice resounds.

But in the Mass of the Faithful there is no preaching. The soul is recollected and expectant, waiting for God, who is hidden under the appearances of bread and wine.

If a typical object may be added to those of the Mass of the Faithful, it is that in which are reserved the additional particles used in the communion of the faithful. These particles are consecrated during Mass together with the Host used by the priest, and they are reserved in the *Ciborium*, a vessel closed tightly by a lid and then covered with a little veil. The word "Ciborium" means a vessel in which food is stored. It is kept hidden in the Tabernacle, a receptacle closed by doors with a lock and key, or bolted and padlocked. There dwells the Most Holy, really and ever present with us.

The open pulpit from which man's speech resounds: the closed Tabernacle where the Body of Christ is reserved: these are what bear witness in the Church to the two different parts of the Mass, as it is celebrated in every Catholic country.

IV

The Mass of the Catechumens

WHEN THE PRIEST actually begins to celebrate Mass, he stands upright at the foot of the three steps, with his face turned towards the altar.

The boy who serves him kneels at the left of the priest.

Then both of them, together with all those present in the church who are going to take part in the Mass, make the Sign of the Cross.

The Sign of the Cross.—Let us remember what the Sign of the Holy Cross meant at the beginning of Christianity.

It was the gesture through which a believer in Christ was recognized by his brothers. It was the sign used by a member of a persecuted society, when the very fact of belonging to it might be punished with cruel death by the powers then ruling.

The password, the word of recognition, was whispered in secret, as an act of faith in the One and Triune God: "In the name of the Father, and of the Son, and of the Holy Ghost." And a sign was made with the right hand, in the form of the Cross, the standard of Christianity: which signified the sacrifice of Christ, the Second Person of the Blessed Trinity.

For almost two thousand years now, Christians have been repeating this sign of victory, and when we make it in our turn we are impressed by its sacred dignity.

The Mass of the Catechumens

So the Mass begins like that; and this great action unites everyone together at the foot of the altar, the officiating priest and the farthest away of those present.

> "In the Name of the Father,
> And of the Son,
> And of the Holy Ghost."

The Mass begins and continues as an act of homage and an offering to the Most Holy Trinity.

The Closed Gate.—When he has made the Sign of the Cross, the priest begins to speak and the boy answers him: you can hear their voices alternating for some minutes.

You would think they were going up the steps any moment, because the phrase is repeated: "I will go unto the altar—I will go unto the altar of God."

But all the same, he does not go.

They are reciting in a low voice some verses of a beautiful psalm, the forty-second, each of them saying a verse in turn. That is why it sounds like a dialogue to those who are listening.

"Introibo ad altare Dei," says the priest (I will go unto the altar of God).

It is no use going up to the altar with an exterior offering, if the heart is not first prepared by an interior offering.

Something like that is taught us by this marvelous Psalm which the priest and the boy (who answers for the people) recite in a dialogue at the foot of the three steps which separate them from the altar.

In that prayer the Psalmist expresses his determination to approach the altar of God. He is sad, but he knows that all joy comes from the Lord. He feels he is persecuted, and he asks justice from God:

"Distinguish," he says, "my cause from the nation that is not holy; deliver me from the unjust and deceitful man."

But his sadness is not lifted. Then he asks God:

"Give me thy light! It will lead me near to Thee and then I shall be happy. I will sing for ever Thy praises, O God of my salvation." But still his soul is disconsolate:

"Why art thou sad, O my soul, and why dost thou disquiet me?"

Repentance.—One would think the priest and the boy were rooted there at the foot of the steps, as though something were holding them back.

No proud man, who thinks he is better than other men, can go up those steps; neither his invocation to the Divine Light nor his promise of praise avail him in the least.

There is only one man who can approach God, and that is the humble, repentant man, who bows down his head and says in sorrow:

"I confess I am a sinner: have mercy on me!"

So all at once the priest is seen to change his attitude. He had been standing upright, but now he bows low down, with his face to the ground, beating his breast with his clenched right hand. Turning towards the boy (who represents the people), he speaks.

"I confess before all," says the priest in effect, "not in secret, but in a loud voice before the public, that I am a sinner; that it is through my fault, through my most grievous fault; and I implore all to help me in invoking the mercy of the Most High. I confess to Almighty God, to the Blessed Virgin Mary, to the Angels, to the Saints, to all men."

Then the boy and all those present bow down their heads too, and likewise confess aloud; and the priest turns to the people as to his brothers, and all the people turn to him as to a father, and they beg each other to pray one for the other, to invoke the Divine mercy and pardon.

The Ascent.—And now at last the priest goes up to the altar. He walks up the three steps of the theological virtues: Faith, Hope, and Charity.

The Meeting with the Saints.—His first encounter is with the holy relics. Moved by reverence and love, the priest bends down and kisses the altar over them.

"By the merits of thy Saints, whose relics lie here, O Lord, pardon all my sins."

The repentant man may pass freely. At last he has reached the altar and has achieved his desire: "I go unto the altar of God, to that God who rejoiceth my youth."

The Open Book.—Turning to the right, he bends over the open Book. The first thing he reads is the "Introit," some verses of a Psalm which are different for every day.

The Kyrie.—At first the priest had simply asked for forgiveness and help, like a man full of sorrow. But now that his desire of going to the altar of God has been granted, his soul is moved and, in the impulse of his heart, he prays aloud a threefold prayer, like a solemn invocation to the Most Holy Trinity: each time he cries out, the boy answers him.

> "Lord, have mercy on us!
> Christ, have mercy on us!
> Lord, have mercy on us!"

The Song of Joy.—Now the priest joins his hands and moves back to the middle of the altar.

He is pervaded with inexpressible joy, with that "joy of

youth" which he had first implored at the foot of the steps. He is happy in God, as the shepherds were that Christmas night when they saw a great light around the stable of Bethlehem, and heard the music of angels proclaiming the birth of the Redeemer.

The same hymn which they sang bursts from his heart:

"Glory be to God in the highest!
And on earth peace to men of good will!
    We praise Thee,
    We bless Thee,
    We adore Thee,
    We glorify Thee,
    We give Thee thanks,
    For Thy great glory.
O Lord God, King of Heaven, God the
    Father Almighty!
O Lord, the only begotten Son, Jesus Christ,
O Lord God, Lamb of God, Son of the Father,
Thou, who takest away the sins of the world,
    Have mercy on us!
Who takest away the sins of the world,
    Receive our prayer.
Who sittest at the right hand of the Father,
    Have mercy on us.
For Thou only art Holy,
Thou only art Lord:
Thou only, O Jesus Christ,
With the Holy Ghost,
Art most high in the glory of God the
    Father. Amen."

The Reading.—Now the priest is silent.

He must read the Epistle, together with the prayers and verses of the Psalms which are proper to the Mass of the day.

But before he begins this special part he turns to the people and addresses them, standing erect at the middle of the altar, to which he turns his back for a second.

"The Lord be with you."

And the people answer him, through the boy's voice:

"And with thy spirit."

Then the priest goes to read out of the holy book, and turns to the right parts for that day.

The Prayers.—First there are short prayers, which are called the "Collects." This word means the prayers collected together. They vary in number according to the feast of the day.

Everyone should listen attentively, with expectant heart, to what is going to be taught him.

Just as a master calls his pupils' special attention before beginning to teach them something difficult and valuable, so the priest bids the congregation to join together, united in heart around him, while he, in the Collects, offers to God the prayers of all those present.

The Epistle.—The next thing read out is called the Epistle, because what was usually read in olden time was some extract from the letters (epistles) written by the first Apostles of Christ, particularly St. Paul and St. Peter. The first Apostles sent instructions and advice to the early Christians who were at a distance from them and who needed to be supported in the Faith, instructed in the Christian virtues, and encouraged to good works; because they needed great perseverance in those days of heavy sacrifice, when the Christians were few, scattered, and often cruelly persecuted.

But often now, under the title of "Epistle," the "Acts of the Apostles" are read out, that is, the story of the heroic or wonderful deeds done by the first followers of Christ, after His death.

And lastly, under the same title, extracts from the Old Testament are often read, referring to the prophecies foretelling Our Lord Jesus Christ, the long-expected Messiah, who had been described in detail by the prophets of Israel, centuries before the Incarnation.

The Scriptures are thus read to us, a little every day, during the whole year. It is like having a teacher, who is at the same time our dear mother, who gives us short, interesting little lessons, always different, to help us to penetrate into holy things. This loving mother and wise teacher is the Church, who has thus arranged what her children are to be taught, dividing it up through the whole liturgical year.

The Gradual.—When he has read what is called the Epistle, the priest reads the Gradual. In ancient times this used to be a hymn from the Psalms, to which the people responded with cries of joy: "Alleluia!" meaning "May the Lord be praised!" The word "Gradual" is taken from the Latin word for step, "gradus"; and the hymn was so called because the early Christians, inflamed with faith, used to come up to the steps of the altar to sing it.

The Gospel.—Now we have come to a very solemn moment.

We have almost come to the words of God; in a few moments we shall hear the teaching of Christ Himself.

Now the religious expectation in our hearts should be intense.

There is a great stir when we are about to hear the divine words. This is the final part of the Mass of the Catechumens. You can imagine them saying: "We have come to listen to the words of the Divine Master! Let us stand up to hear."

The Book, which was at the right side of the altar, is carried to the left, to show how different is the voice of God from that of men.

The priest feels unworthy of this task of transmitting the words of Our Lord. He would wish to be worthy, to be made pure. So you see him stop at the middle of the altar, with his head bowed, to address to God that most ardent and beautiful prayer, the *Munda Car Meum...* "Cleanse my heart and my lips, O Almighty God, who didst cleanse with a burning coal the lips of the Prophet Isaias!" Then he goes to the left.

Now he stands before the Book, open at the Gospel which the Church has ordered to be read on that day.

Then the priest speaks to the people to call their attention; but they are already standing and filled with the great solemnity of the moment, waiting to make the Sign of the Cross three times with the priest.

"The Lord be with you," says the priest.

"And with thy spirit," they answer.

Then he commences reading:

"The continuation of the Holy Gospel..."

He makes the Sign of the Cross on the Book and then a little Cross on his forehead, on his lips and on his breast, to sanctify his thoughts, words and actions before reading the Gospel for the day. The people, too, make these three crosses, and the boy says: "Glory be to Thee, O Lord." When the priest finishes, the boy's voice is heard exclaiming: "Praise be to thee, O Christ!" while the priest devoutly kisses the Book, saying: "By the words of the Gospel may our sins be blotted out!"

The Creed.—After the preaching of Christ, what should we do?

Proclaim our faith in a loud voice. The priest goes to the middle of the altar and begins to recite the Creed, and all those present, standing, follow his words.

Only at the sentence: "And was incarnate," priest and people go down on the right knee and remain devoutly kneeling until the words: "And was made Man," when they stand up again until the end of the Creed. The final Amen this time does not mean the usual invocation "So be it," but it is an affirmation of the truth: "So it is." And now the priest, with a *Dominus vobiscum,* announces that the Mass of the Catechumens is over.

V
The Mass of the Faithful

THE OFFERTORY

IN OLDEN TIMES, as we have seen, the Catechumens went away after that *Dominus vobiscum,* which was their farewell salutation; because only the initiated, that is, Christians already instructed and baptized, were allowed to be present at the Mass of the Faithful.

Numbers of the faithful now brought their offerings up to the altar. During this coming and going alms were asked for the poorer brethren and the names of benefactors were read out. But all the bustle was covered by the singing of a Psalm intoned in chorus. This varied from day to day and came to be called the Offertory.

Little remains now of that ancient scene. Those who do not know the Mass hardly notice this passage, except perhaps on a Sunday, if offerings are collected at this time. Then you will see a number of people going round the church with a plate or a bag in their hands, or perhaps carrying the bag at the end of a long stick, to collect offerings from the congregation. This is the last vestige of a very ancient custom. And instead of the Psalm, which was sung in its entirety in olden days, only three little verses are read in the present-day rite, and these vary according to the Mass for the day. This is called the *Offertory* of the day. The priest turns to read it out of the Missal at the left, and then returns to the middle of the altar.

The first thing he does now is to uncover that mysterious wrapping, which has been left standing all this time on that part of the altar over the holy stone.

Usually at the beginning of Mass he has taken the Burse and put it at the left-hand side, resting it upright carefully, after having taken out the Corporal and spread it on the altar stone. He now takes off the Veil and puts it at the right side. The Chalice now stands uncovered save for the Pall and Paten. He takes off the Pall, puts it on his right, and reverently lifting the Paten with the Host on it, he offers the Host to God, saying: "Receive, O my God, this spotless Host. . . ."

With the Paten he makes a small Sign of the Cross, and then tipping it, lets the Host slip on to the Corporal. Then he puts the Paten a little to the side.

Now for the Chalice, which is empty.

The priest wipes it first with the Purificator, and then moves with it to the right of the altar. The server is standing there ready with the cruets in his hand; the priest pours the wine into the Chalice and adds a little water, blessing it and praying: "O God, who in creating man didst exalt his nature very wonderfully and yet more wonderfully didst form it anew, grant that by the mystery of this water and wine we may become sharers in His Divinity, who did not disdain to share in our humanity."

The priest then offers the Chalice, holding it raised up a little from the Corporal: "We offer up to Thee, O Lord, the Chalice of Salvation." Then, having traced with it the Sign of the Cross, he puts it down where it was before and covers it with the Pall.

Now the bread and wine, not yet consecrated, have been offered up.

The priest stands absorbed and bowed a little, with his eyes fixed on them, and his hands joined, resting on the edge of the altar. He recalls how a man's soul must be prepared if it is to reach God:

"Humbled in mind and contrite of heart, may we find favor with Thee, O Lord."

Then you will see him raise his head. He unclasps his two hands, then raises them up as if they, too, were drawn towards heaven, and looking upward a moment in supplication to the Holy Ghost, he says:

"Come, Thou the Sanctifier, God Almighty and Everlasting, and bless this Sacrifice."

As he says the last words, with his hands he blesses the bread and wine.

In a few minutes these hands will touch the Body of Christ!

Just as he prayed that his lips should be purified, before he read the Gospel, so now he feels the need of purifying his hands.

He goes to the right. There, the boy is ready with the cruet of water, the dish, and the finger-towel, and he pours a little water over the priest's fingers.

While the priest washes them, he says a psalm containing these words, and others:

"I will wash my hands among the innocent: O Lord, I have loved the beauty of Thy house! Take not away my soul, O God. Glory be to the Father, and to the Son, and to the Holy Ghost."

He returns to the center.

It is to the Blessed Trinity he makes the offering, and he must state it formally and express his intention:

"Receive, O Holy Trinity, this oblation offered up by us to Thee, in memory of the Passion, Resurrection, and Ascension of Our Lord Jesus Christ. . . ."

Now, he must remember the great souls of the Saints. Yes, we wish our offering to be in their honor, in honor of the Blessed Virgin Mary and the Saints. We remember them on earth that they may in their loving-kindness intercede for us when the great moment comes.

That is what the priest prays for, with his head bowed and his hands joined.

The people wait in silence.

And see, the priest does not forget them. When he has kissed the altar, he turns to them, saying:

"Pray, my brothers, that this sacrifice, both mine and yours, may be acceptable to God the Father Almighty."

The boy hastens to reply, in the name of all present: "May the Lord receive this Sacrifice from thy hands, to the praise and glory of His name, for our good likewise, and for that of all His holy Church."

Both the priest and the boy say those prayers out loud.

Then they are silent. The "Amen" which the priest answers can hardly be heard. When the priest goes to the Book, he reads the "Secret Prayers" in a voice which cannot be heard at all.

The offering which he now makes may be secretly repeated for himself by each one present. Since the bread and wine have been offered . . . well, let us offer our hearts too. So each one, in silence, makes an offering of himself; and in that moment of silence, it is as though altar and people were lifted up together, beseeching Heaven.

THE CENTER OF THE MASS

THE CONSECRATION is the center of the whole Mass and is so solemn that it begins with a Preface, that is, with a kind of preparation or act of welcome.

The moment of consecration, or the Sacrifice, follows later.

That moment, in which the words of the Last Supper are spoken and the Living Christ descends, commemorates the Passion, and particularly that time in the life of the Messiah when He offered Himself for us in sacrifice on the Cross. The center of the whole action is the sacrifice, and therefore this word gives its name to the whole Mass: The Holy Sacrifice of the Mass.

First, however, there is a salutation to honor and glorify the Messiah, just as really happened in history, when Jesus was made welcome in Jerusalem by the hosannas, and greeted with branches of palm: "Hosanna! Hosanna! Blessed is He that cometh in the name of the Lord!"

The Preface (or the Hosanna).—In the rite of Mass, the beginning of the Preface is signaled by the priest's raising his voice.

He had been reading the Secret in silence, and he ends up a prayer, which he had begun to himself, by saying in a loud voice:

"World without end, Amen."

The people are roused out of their silent meditation. They hear the priest giving them that greeting, which nearly always means that he wants to call their special attention:

Dominus vobiscum!

Then the priest cries:

"Lift up your hearts!"

"Ah," the boy answers him gladly, "we have them already lifted up to God!"

Priest and people are all penetrated with the same joy; He is about to arrive!

"Let us then give thanks to God," says the priest, who feels the need of expressing his gratitude and saluting the

Lord. And in this thanksgiving he wants the people to support him, and to share with him.

"It is meet and just!" the boy answers.

The priest goes on:

"It is truly meet and just, right and profitable for us, at all times, and in all places, to give thanks to Thee, O Holy Lord, Father Almighty, Everlasting God, through Jesus Christ Our Lord . . . Through Whom Angels praise Thy Majesty, Dominations adore it, and the Powers tremble with awe before it . . . while the Blessed Seraphim rejoice in it with one voice. O Lord, we beseech Thee, command that it be permitted to our lowliness to join our voices with them. . . ."

Immediately the boy reaches out his hand to the bell and rings it strongly in token of solemnity; and all the people kneel down, joining with the priest in calling out salutations to the Lord:

"Holy! Holy! Holy! Lord God of Hosts!
The heavens and the earth are full of Thy glory!
Hosanna in the Highest!
Blessed is he that cometh in the name of the Lord!
Hosanna in the Highest!"

SACRIFICE

The Ancient Rite.—The central part of the Mass of the Faithful which is now about to begin and is called "The Sacrifice," corresponds with and for ever replaces the old rites of pagan religions, and also the religion of the Chosen Race.

These rites were made up not only of prayers, but also of "offerings" to the divinity, to whom a gift—a material present—was offered. But since the people could not in reality give anything to an invisible god, something was made over in his honor, and usually some live animal was killed: the victim of the holocaust (a word meaning "whole burnt offering"). This was done with great solemnity when the chosen victim had been made over to the god on a high place or altar.

This action of making something sacred was called the sacrifice. And since the action was carried out on an altar, it was, therefore, called the sacrifice of the altar. In ordinary language, the word "sacrifice" has taken on the meaning of "giving up," since the object presented to the divinity represented a privation felt by those who offered it: for always the most worthy and dearest thing was offered. The Bible tells us about Abel, the just man, who sacrificed to God the most beautiful lamb of his flock; and it shows us Abraham, the patriarch, who was ready to obey God at once, when he was ordered to sacrifice his only son, because no sacrifice ever seemed to him sufficiently worthy of God. It was the function of the priest in the Old Law to make the victim sacred by imposing his hands upon it and stretching them out over it. (In Latin, the consecrated victim was called *hostia*, the host.)

The act of consecration was carried out with striking ceremonies and great pomp. Then followed the slaying, the sacred animal being usually killed in such a way that its blood was shed.

The object of offering up a victim on the altar was to make an act of homage to God, and also to appease Him if He had been offended, and to conciliate Him so as to obtain His protection.

These religious customs may seem surprising to us Christians, and yet they were the expression of a feeling very natural to man. Even in ordinary life, somewhat similar offerings are often made: for example, when we cut off a beautiful flower with a pair of scissors and offer it to someone in homage, we are making a victim because we cut short the life of the flower. If we wish to show honor to a great personage, we look for the rarest, most sweet-smelling flowers, and we set them off by wrapping them in pretty paper or silk and tying them with showy ribbons. The person who makes the offering dresses specially for the occasion and studies beforehand the right gestures and the curtsey proper for presenting the offering.

You can understand that the same desire was expressed with much more wealth and magnificence when the offering was made to an omnipotent God.

The New Rite.—It was Jesus who taught us a richer doctrine, surpassing the ideal based on human instincts, a doctrine coming from on high and full of divine wisdom.

Christ showed us that God wants something greater than holocausts.

One only sacrifice is offered, and that is of the Son of Man for our sake. Our sacrifice is to offer that same Victim, uniting ourselves to Him, giving our whole hearts as a gift with Him.

As a matter of fact, what is a holocaust? It is a sign, and its only value is its *meaning* of devotion and homage. But if the person receiving it is our king and absolute master, he cannot be content with it. What a king desires is that his subjects should love him, that they should be faithful to him, that they should labor to produce riches and monuments, immortal works; in short, that they should build up a powerful kingdom.

63

Jesus offered Himself in sacrifice, in the very way God had ordained and willed, down to the last detail: and in doing this, He was obedient to the Father even unto death, even unto the death of the Cross.

Ah! In those hours when the Blood of Jesus was poured out on Golgotha, the whole world was an altar: and yet one single drop of that Blood would have been enough to wash away all the crimes of the world.

The Mass of the present day represents the sacrifice of the altar and the offering up of a victim in conciliation, by the shedding of its blood. This offering is made to God, who has cause to be angered by the sins of men; and the offering is made to adore Him and to thank Him, to appease Him and to obtain mercy, grace, and blessing.

But in the new rite the victim is always Jesus Christ, who offers Himself in sacrifice for us, that He may redeem us so fully as to make us partakers in His Divinity. In the new rite the Host is the consecrated Bread—the Living Body of Christ.

The Mass perpetually re-presents the sacrifice in that moment when Our Lord comes upon the altar under the appearance of the bread and wine: and the Elevation of the Host and Chalice represents His Elevation on the Cross.

The Canon.—The ceremonies of the sacrifice of the altar have been laid down by laws governing the rite and ceremonial of the Mass.

And particularly in this mystical part of the sacrifice and offering, every single action is prescribed. That is why this central part of the rite is called the "Canon," a word which means "Rule."

The action representing the Last Supper takes first place

in the rite. That scene is repeated by the priest, who represents Christ, and when he repeats the actions and words, there is the same effect: the bread and wine become Our Lord's Body and Blood.

"Sing, O my tongue, the mystery of the glorious Body, and the precious Blood, which the King of all nations shed as the price of the world.

"In the night of the Last Supper, when seated at table with His brethren . . . the Word Incarnate, by a word, made real bread become His Flesh, and made the wine become the Blood of Christ. And if our senses cannot understand how such a prodigy can be renewed, Faith alone is enough to convince a sincere heart.

"Let us bow down in adoration of such a Sacrament, wherein the ancient forms give place to the new rite."

The Diptychs.—In the Canon of the Mass, certain prayers are said to recommend the living and the dead to God and to ask the saints for the help of their prayers and merits. Now, to make clear the central part of the Mass of the Faithful, you must distinguish such prayers from what strictly refers to the offering and the sacrifice of the altar. These prayers are called diptychs, because in ancient times diptychs (or folding tablets of wood, metal or ivory) were used for registering in a long list the names of living or dead people whom one wanted to mention in the "Memento of the Living" and the "Memento of the Dead."

For invoking the Saints, too, a long list of proper names occurs.

This custom is a proof of love and great faith. The Lord is about to come; He who said to us: "Ask and it shall be given unto you."

While the priest invokes Him with that power which comes to him from the promise of Christ, and while he follows out the ritual established in the Canon, it is natural that the people (and the priest himself) should come forward to ask graces for themselves and for those they love in this life; and that they should implore mercy from Him who descended into Limbo to obtain the deliverance and peace of the souls of those who had died in His faith.

In Palestine, too, when Our Lord was passing by, many used to come round Him to ask Him to cure someone who was not present, like the centurion who asked Him to save his dying servant, or Mary and Martha, who besought Him to raise Lazarus from the dead.

When we truly believe that it is the same Living Christ who comes to us mystically in the Mass, we are immediately inspired to ask for things, exactly as the people did whom He met during His life on earth.

In consideration of such feelings, these petitions are permitted in the rite of Mass. During the "Memento of the Living," which occurs almost at the beginning of the Canon, and the "Memento of the Dead," which occurs towards the end of it, all present recommend and name those dear to them and the people for whom they want to pray. This is done in the deepest silence and stillness.

In the same way, mentioning the Blessed Virgin Mary and a long list of Saints by name is an act of spiritual union inspired by faith. Because in great moments of our life we feel ourselves united to people we know, as though our memory were illuminated to enable us to distinguish these persons separately.

Something very much the same happens in worldly affairs.

If a crowd is waiting for the arrival of some great personage, a stir runs through them when he comes, and people belonging to the same family call each other by name and push forward. Then everyone looks hard to see if they know anyone among the people in authority, and if they do they call out to their acquaintance to ask some privilege, perhaps for a better place where they can see the great person more closely.

The prayers of the diptychs are a very special sharing of the congregation in the Mass of the Faithful. Now, you will not hear the boy answer the priest, only he kneels closer to him and holds the bell ready, because that is the only voice now that may ring out in the church.

It all takes place between the priest and God in a mysterious colloquy.

The priest does not now move from the middle of the altar; the book is near him, placed slantwise at the left, so that he can read from it without moving.

The hands of the priest, in their gestures, express more than words, since words are no longer heard. The priest murmurs inaudibly, now raising his eyes to heaven, now looking down on the offerings, which, however, he never touches until the moment of the consecration. His hands are raised up nearly all the time, motionless and apart, in an act of invocation; or they are joined in prayer. In contrast with the immobility and tension of the hands when praying, you see them repeatedly making a rapid Sign of the Cross over the offerings. These gestures are like God's answer in this mysterious dialogue. The man invokes and prays; and God blesses.

The Consecration.—We left the priest after the Sanctus, standing upright and motionless at the center of the altar, before the Host and Chalice which he has just presented as an offering, raising them up a little from the Corporal.

But now he does not touch them. The solemn gestures of his hands seem to invoke on them the divine blessing.

He throws out his hands and immediately joins them; raises his eyes to heaven and then lowers them. Lastly he ponders, bending low over the altar and resting his hands upon it.

Te Igitur: "Wherefore, most Merciful Father, we very humbly beg and beseech Thee, through Jesus Christ. . . ."

At that name he bends his head still lower, and kisses the altar; and his hands, which had been resting on it, he now joins before his breast:

". . . to receive and to bless. . . ." Then immediately he moves his right hand and makes three little crosses over the offerings,
". . . these gifts, these oblations, these holy and spotless hosts."

Now he opens his hands and holds them out wide in a gesture of solemn invocation.

Then comes that insertion, which we have already noted, of the "Memento of the Living" and the *Communicantes* (Commemoration of the Saints).

The offerings remain exposed there, waiting.

The priest knows that what is soon to become the Victim is lying there on the Corporal to be offered up. And just as the high priests did in the ancient rites, when they consecrated the victim on the altar, he imposes his hands, holding them out motionless over the Host and the Chalice.

"Wherefore, we beseech Thee, O Lord, to be appeased by this Oblation which we, Thy servants, and with us Thy whole family, offer to Thee, and to receive it . . . that we may be numbered in the flock of Thine elect."

The white Host and the wine in the Chalice are set out ready on this mystical table just as, so many centuries ago now, the bread and wine were put ready on the table of the Last Supper, waiting to be consecrated by the word of Christ.

The same scene will be repeated in a moment: and the priest will have the same power!

But first he asks God to make the offerings worthy of the great change about to take place:

"Do thou, O God, in all ways vouchsafe to *bless* this same Oblation, to *take* it for Thy very own, to *approve* it, to perfect it, and to render it well-pleasing to Thyself, so that, on our behalf, it may be changed into the *Body* and *Blood* of Jesus Christ, Thy most dear Son, our Lord."

Every desire expressed by word is accompanied by the blessing of the Cross; first three crosses are made over the Host and Chalice together, then one only over the Host and one only over the Chalice (at the words italicized).

And now the scene of the Last Supper is beginning. The priest relates it in the words of the Gospel and actually carries out the first gestures of it.

"Who [that is, Thy most dear Son] the day before He suffered [the priest takes the Host into his hands] took bread into His holy and venerable hands. [The priest raises his eyes to heaven.] . . . and having lifted up His eyes to heaven, to Thee, God, His Almighty Father [The priest bends his head in salutation], giving thanks to Thee. . . . [Taking the Host in his left hand, he makes the Sign of the Cross over it with his right hand.] . . . He blessed it, broke it, and gave it to His disciples, saying: Take ye, and eat ye all of this."

Now the priest holds the Host between the first finger and thumb of each hand and bends down, pronouncing his words one by one very slowly:

"FOR THIS IS MY BODY."

When the priest has said these words, he kneels, adoring the Sacred Body of Christ. The bell is rung in the deep silence of the people.

Then rising, the priest elevates the Host on high, that all present may see It and breathe with him:

"My Lord and my God!"

The boy reverently lifts the hem of his chasuble to take the weight off his shoulders and leave his arms free to move. The bell rings again.

The priest rests the Consecrated Host on the Corporal; but those fingers that held it, the thumb and first finger of both hands, remain pressed together as though they could

never again be separated. He kneels and again adores: and again the bell rings.

He uncovers the Chalice, putting the Pall to one side, and resumes the scene of the Last Supper.

"In like manner, after they had supped [the priest takes the Chalice with both hands, but still never separating the thumb from the first finger of each hand], taking also into His holy and venerable hands this goodly Chalice . . . again [the priest bows his head] giving thanks to Thee [supporting the raised Chalice in his left hand, he makes the Sign of the Cross in blessing over it with his right hand] He blessed it . . . and gave it to His disciples, saying: Take ye, and drink ye all of this."

Now, holding up the Chalice slightly, the priest says over it the words of consecration carefully and without pause, but separating each word from the others:

"FOR THIS IS THE CHALICE OF MY BLOOD, OF THE NEW AND EVERLASTING TESTAMENT, THE MYSTERY OF FAITH, WHICH FOR YOU AND FOR MANY SHALL BE SHED, FOR THE REMISSION OF SINS."

He rests the Sacred Chalice on the Corporal.

The priest has had the same power as Jesus: what is now in the Chalice is the Blood of Christ, the very same that dropped down on Golgotha, bathing the wood of the Holy Cross.

"As often as ye do these things, ye shall do them in memory of Me," says the priest silently. Then he kneels and adores the Precious Blood and rises immediately and elevates the Chalice on high, that all present may see and adore It.

When he has laid It down again on the Corporal, he covers It with the Pall, kneels, and again adores.

The boy, bowed down in adoration, has again taken hold of the hem of the priest's chasuble; and he rings the bell three times as before, so that it resounds in every heart like a commemoration of the sacrifice of Christ.

The Consecration is over...

The Offering.—The moment has come to offer to the Eternal Father the Host which is to appease and conciliate the Divine Majesty.

When making the offering, the priest commemorates Christ, as He commanded:

"Wherefore, O Lord, bearing in mind the blessed Passion of the same Christ, Thy Son, our Lord, His Resurrection likewise from the grave, and His glorious Ascension into Heaven, we, too, Thy servants—nay, rather, Thy holy people—offer up to Thine excellent Majesty from among the things Thou hast given to us and bestowed upon us, a Victim pure, a Victim holy, a Victim stainless. . . ."

As he says this, the priest makes the Sign of the Cross three times over the Chalice and the Host together. Then, distinguishing between the two different Species, under each of which the whole of Christ is contained, he makes a single Sign of the Cross over the Host, saying: "The holy Bread of life everlasting," and one over the Chalice, saying: "And the Cup of eternal salvation."

Separating his hands, he implores acceptance of the Offerings, recalling all the Just, the Patriarchs and Priests who offered their holocausts to God from the beginning of time.

"Vouchsafe to look upon them with a gracious and tranquil countenance, and to accept them, even as Thou was pleased to accept the offerings of Thy righteous servant, Abel, the sacrifice of Abraham, our Patriarch, and that which Melchisedech, Thy high priest, offered up to Thee, a holy sacrifice, a spotless host."

He bows down so deeply that his forehead almost touches the altar; then he rests his joined hands on the edge of the altar and says:

"Humbly, we beseech Thee, Almighty God, to command that by the hands of Thy holy Angel, this our Sacrifice be uplifted to Thine Altar on high, into the very presence of Thy Divine Majesty, and to grant that as many of us [here he kisses the altar] as, by this partaking of the Altar, shall have received the adorable Body and Blood of Thy Son [he makes the Sign of the Cross once over the Host and once over the Chalice, then over himself, saying:] may from heaven be filled with all blessing and grace [he joins his hands]. Through the same Christ our Lord. Amen."

Reflecting on the plenitude of graces and blessings poured down on those present at the Mass, he is reminded of those who can no longer take part in it. He prays for the dead, who are waiting in longing expectation and burning desire of God, but who cannot yet reach Him. His heart is moved, especially when he remembers his own dead. All the faithful join silently in this act of petition for the dead, the second of the Diptychs.

Then suddenly you hear the priest's voice raised a little. His hands which, whether joined or parted, had all this time been in an attitude of prayer, remind you now of that repentant man at the foot of the altar, because he beats his breast with his right hand:

"Nobis quoque peccatoribus!" "On ourselves, too, who are sinners. . . ."

It is as if the man who has been immersed in God and forgetful of himself suddenly brings his attention back to himself, acknowledging that he is a sinner.

But then, recollecting the need of great respect, he goes back to the low-voiced murmur of the prayers, making petition for himself and for all those present. He asks for a great deal, because in the presence of the King one can ask for much. All those present at Mass are almost in the position of the first Apostles, who gathered closely round Our Lord in intimacy, surrounding Him while He talked to them of the Kingdom of Heaven.

"On us, who put our trust in the multitude of Thy tender mercies, deign to bestow some place and fellowship with Thy saints…"

And he mentions these by name:

"With thy holy Apostles and Martyrs, with John, Stephen, Matthias, Barnabas, Ignatius, Alexander, Marcellinus, Peter; Felicity, Perpetua, Agatha, Lucy, Agnes, Cecilia, Anastasia, and all Thy saints."

And he justifies himself for this greatest of all requests by adding:

"We beseech Thee, not weighing our merits but freely pardoning us our sins."

The faithful will not be rebuked, like the sons of Zebedee, for having made this request. True, they have asked for the greatest thing of all, but not the impossible. We may all aspire to holiness; indeed, it is to attain it that we seek for union with Christ. He became Man and continually returns among us, uniquely for this: to lead us to the Kingdom of Heaven, to the glory of the Blessed Trinity.

The very loftiest aspirations are made possible by the merits of Christ, so he adds: *Per Christum Dominum nostrum*—"through Christ our Lord,"

> "By whom, O Lord, Thou dost, at all times, create, hallow, quicken, bless [here again the priest makes the threefold Sign of the Cross] and bestow upon us all these good things. . . ."

Then he uncovers the Chalice, putting the Pall aside to accomplish the last action of the great mystical ceremonial.

He takes the Host between the thumb and first finger of his right hand and the Chalice with his left (but always keeping pressed together the two fingers of this hand that had held the Sacred Host) and once more, while he says the words:

> "Through Him, and with Him, and in Him,"

he makes the Sign of the Cross three times, slowly, with the Host over the Chalice, from one edge of the cup to the other.

Then, still with the Host, he makes the Sign of the Cross twice between the Chalice and his own breast:

> ". . . is to Thee, who art God, the Father Almighty, in the unity of the Holy Ghost, all honor and all glory."

While he is saying these last words, he slightly raises the Chalice with the Host on it. Laying them down again on the Corporal in the usual place, he covers the Chalice with the Pall, and genuflects.

Then in a clear, audible voice he calls out to all present that the beatitude to which we aspire is everlasting:

Per omnia saecula saeculorum. "World without end."

"*Amen,*" cries the boy, as though to show that he and the people have been united with the priest in everything he has done and said from the beginning to the end.

After requesting such great grace, a final prayer must be offered up.

Who could compose a prayer worthy of such a great moment? Only Christ Himself.

"Let us pray," exhorts the priest, his hands now joined.

"Thereto admonished by wholesome precepts, and in words commanded us by God Himself, we dare to say:

'Our Father, who art in heaven,
Hallowed be Thy name,
Thy kingdom come,
Thy will be done,
On earth as it is in heaven.
Give us this day our daily bread;
And forgive us our trespasses,
As we forgive them that trespass against us.
And lead us not into temptation.'"

And the boy's voice takes it up, crying out:
"But deliver us from evil." To which the priest silently answers: *Amen.*

PEACE

IN THE LAST SUPPER, after the consecration of the bread
and wine, Our Lord waited while His disciples obeyed His
command: "Drink ye and eat ye all of this." The Most
Sacred Chalice was passed round from lip to lip, and even
Judas drank of it; then the Bread was divided, and each of
the Apostles took a piece of it.

The action in the last part of the Mass of the Faithful is
the very same.

In the Mass of the Faithful, which is a copy of the Last
Supper, the great ceremonial of the consecration of the
Host and the Wine has now ended, that part of the mysti-
cal action closing with the recital of the Pater Noster.

The people, through the mouth of the boy, had prayed:
"Deliver us from evil": because the action which the priest
and the faithful are now preparing for will have a twofold
effect, according as those who receive it work for good or
for evil, whether in word or in deed.

He who dares to receive the communion of Jesus while
in mortal sin shall have no more peace: like Judas, he shall
taste of eternal death. But the good who eat the Bread of
angels shall taste the perfect Peace that is found in the
Kingdom of Heaven.

"Deliver us, we beseech Thee, O Lord, from all evils,
past, present and to come . . ." says the priest in an under-
tone. He has taken the Paten between the first and second
fingers of his right hand: it is the plate from which he is
now preparing to eat at the Sacred Table; but all this time
those fingers—the thumb and first finger—which have
held the Body of Christ, may not be separated. He continues the prayer in a low voice: "and by the intercession of the
Blessed and Glorious Mary, ever a Virgin, Mother of God,

of Thy holy Apostles Peter and Paul, of Andrew, and of all Thy Saints. . . ." Here he makes the Sign of the Cross, and since he is holding the Paten, he makes it with the Paten; "of Thy loving kindness, grant peace in our time. . . ."

He is asking for the peace that can come to us only through communion with Christ. Then he kisses the Paten, remembering that it is the plate from which his soul shall receive the food of angels; ". . . so that in the help Thy mercy shall afford us, we may all the days of our life find both freedom from sin and safety in every trouble."

Preparation for Holy Communion.—The priest now begins to make the preparations for receiving the Body and Blood of Our Lord. He accompanies the first actions with the three succeeding parts of the prayer in honor of the Blessed Trinity, which returns so often to his lips:

"Through the same Jesus Christ, Thy Son, Our Lord, Who liveth and reigneth with Thee in the unity of the Holy Ghost, World without end."

In his first action the priest slips the Paten under the Host on the Corporal, and uncovers the Chalice, putting the Pall to one side. On the Corporal, therefore, there is now the Paten containing the Host and the uncovered Chalice. Then he takes the Host from the Paten with the

first finger and thumb of each hand, just as he did for the Elevation: but now he does not elevate It; he holds It over the Chalice with both hands and breaks It in two, saying the first part of that prayer: "Through the same Jesus Christ, Thy Son, Our Lord."

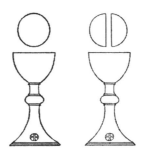

Even if you are a fairly long distance from the altar, you can hear the noise of that breaking of the Host, and it is profoundly impressive to those who love the Mass. They seem to be present at the cruel deed of that soldier who pierced with a lance the heart of Christ! But breaking the Host does not divide the living Body of Our Lord.

After this, he replaces on the Paten the right half of the Host; then with his free hand, he breaks off a fragment of the Host from the left half, keeping it between the first finger and thumb of his right hand.

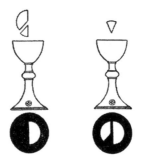

While performing the second action, the priest says the second part of the prayer: "Who liveth and reigneth with Thee in the unity of the Holy Ghost."

Then with his left hand, he lays down on the Paten the remaining part of the Host, alongside the complete half which is there already, and holding the fragment in his right hand over the Chalice, he completes the prayer, raising his voice: "World without end."

The boy again answers: *Amen.*

Now the priest addresses the people:

Pax Domini sit semper vobiscum. (The peace of the Lord be ever with you.)

As he says these words, the priest makes the threefold Sign of the Cross with that little particle of the Host over the Chalice. Through the mouth of the boy, the people fervently unite with the priest in his wish for peace:

"And with thy spirit."

Then the priest drops the fragment of the Host into the Chalice, silently saying this prayer:

"May this commingling and consecrating of the Body and Blood of Our Lord Jesus Christ be to us who shall receive It unto life everlasting."

Then he covers the Chalice and genuflects before the Sacred Species, which are now ready for the mystical banquet.

The priest stops and meditates for an instant; then he beats his breast three times, asking mercy and peace. He knows that it is no longer merely the altar which he approaches, as at the *Confiteor*, but he must receive God Himself, in the Communion of the Body and Blood, Soul and Divinity of Christ:

> "Lamb of God, who takest away the sins of the world,"
> the priest twice exclaims aloud, "have mercy on us!"
> "Lamb of God, who takest away the sins of the world,
> grant us peace!"

The marvelous gift he is about to receive will be life or death to him, according as he is good or wicked. But his heart burns with desire to be united with Our Lord. Like a panting hart running to the fountain of water, so his soul runs towards God; he loves this spiritual food with the hunger of a new-born babe.

But, before proceeding to carry out the sublime act, he prays God first to grant peace to the whole Church, then to prepare his heart to receive Him worthily. With his hands joined and resting on the altar, he bows down, saying silently:

"Lord Jesus Christ, who didst say to Thine Apostles:
'Peace I leave you,
My peace I give unto you';
look not upon my sins but upon the faith of Thy
    Church,
and according to Thy will
deign to give her peace and unity in herself...
Thou who by Thy death hast given life to the world,
free me from all my wickedness and from every evil...
Suffer not that at any time I be separated from Thee...
Let not the partaking of Thy Body,
which I, all unworthy, presume to receive,
turn to my judgment and condemnation;
but, do Thou, in Thy loving kindness,
make it to avail me to my healing and safekeeping in
    body and in soul."

He genuflects before the Blessed Sacrament of the altar and then declares what he is about to do: "I will take the Bread of heaven and will call upon the name of the Lord."

The Priest's Communion.—Bending a little, he takes both parts of the Host which are resting on the Paten between the thumb and first finger of his left hand; he keeps the Paten between the first and second fingers of the same hand, so that it may be always under the Host, for fear some tiny fragment might fall and get lost. Then he beats his breast three times with his right hand, repeating thrice the humble prayer of that centurion full of faith, who besought from Jesus the miracle of curing his sick servant in the house, without going in, because his house was not fit to receive Him: "Say but the word and my servant shall be healed!"

As the priest repeats this prayer, he says aloud only the first words, which all the people hear: "Lord! I am not worthy." And each time he continues in a low voice that phrase which pleased Our Lord Himself so much: ". . . that Thou shouldst enter into my house, but say only the word and my soul shall be healed!" Then he crosses himself with the Host, holding It over the Paten with his right hand, and says: "May the Body of Our Lord Jesus Christ keep my soul unto life everlasting. Amen." And bowing down, he reverently eats the two parts of the Host.

Replacing the empty Paten on the Corporal, he joins his hands and meditates for a few seconds on the Most Holy Sacrament, which is now no longer on the altar, but enclosed within him, as in a Tabernacle.

Then, knowing that Jesus is whole and entire in every least particle of the Host, he moves the Paten all around on the Corporal, as if to collect the minutest remains of the Sacred Host. Then he proceeds to purify that shining, gold Paten, now completely empty. Holding it aslant over the Chalice, he brushes it all round carefully with his finger, as if to cast into the Chalice all that his finger can remove. While he is carrying out this task, he says:

"What shall I render unto the Lord for all the good things He has rendered unto me?
"I will take the Chalice of salvation and will call upon the name of the Lord. With praises will I call upon the Lord, and I shall be safe from mine enemies."

Then he takes the Chalice in his right hand and crosses

himself with it, saying: "May the Blood of our Lord Jesus Christ keep my soul unto life everlasting. Amen."

Whereupon, holding the Paten under the Chalice with his left hand, so that it would receive the least drop that might fall, he reverently takes all the Blood with the particle of the Host contained in it.

The Communion of the Faithful.—Our Lord has come down on the altar, through the action of the priest, and He has come for all.

At the Last Supper there were only the twelve Apostles to receive His Sacred Body, but after His glorious resurrection and ascension all humanity can share in Him throughout the centuries. And so the faithful who are in a state of grace are allowed to approach the altar. At this moment, the ineffable mystery of the union between God and man is about to take place. No one will be turned away, because all are called: men, women, the old and the young.

Keep in mind what is needed to open the gates of God: humility; a contrite heart. So now, all the faithful repeat that same confession which the priest made before he could go up the steps of the altar. Devoutly and recollectedly, with their hands joined, they walk up to the altar rail, while the boy says the *Confiteor* for them all.

When he comes to the words: "Through my fault..." they beat their breasts as an act of contrition.

At the end of the *Confiteor* the priest gives them absolution, blessing them with the Sign of the Cross.

Meanwhile, he has opened the Tabernacle to take out the Ciborium, which he uncovers. Then he takes a Particle in his hand, showing It to those kneeling before the altar, and saying as a sort of invitation:

"Behold the Lamb of God!
"Behold Him who takes away the sins of the world!"

Then, on behalf of the people, he repeats the centurion's prayer:

"Lord, I am not worthy that Thou shouldst enter under my roof; but say only the word, and my soul shall be healed."

And they beat their breasts three times, as the priest did when he said this prayer for himself.

Now they are ready to take part in the mystical banquet; the priest passes along, stopping before each one to give him a Particle, with this greeting of great comfort:

"May the Body of our Lord Jesus Christ keep thy soul unto life everlasting. Amen."

"And when they had sung a hymn they went forth."—These words conclude in the Gospel the description of the Last Supper. Likewise in the Mass the faithful rise up again and retire to their places, and the priest says certain prayers, which all may repeat in their hearts. First he says: "With a pure heart, O Lord, may we receive the Heavenly Food which has passed our lips; bestowed upon us in time, may it be our healing for eternity."

Then he proceeds to purify his hands, which have touched Christ's Body, and the Chalice which has held His Blood. He holds out the Chalice to the boy at the right-hand side of the altar, and the boy pours in wine, which the priest drinks. Then he prays that the Grace of God may penetrate his whole soul:

"May Thy Body, O Lord, of which I have eaten, and

Thy Blood, of which I have drunk, cleave to mine inmost parts: and do Thou grant that no stain of sin remain in me, whom Thou hast comforted with Thy pure and holy Sacraments."

Taking up the Chalice, and holding over it the thumbs and first fingers of both hands (those fingers which have never parted except to hold the Sacred Host), he allows the boy to pour over them wine and water. He drinks this mixture containing the last trace of the Sacrament which his fingers had touched, and now at last he separates these fingers and wipes them. Finally, he wipes his mouth and the Chalice with the purificator, puts the purificator over the top of the Chalice, the Paten on top of the purificator, and the Pall on top of the Paten; he folds up the Corporal and puts it in the Burse, and puts everything back in the middle of the altar as it was at the beginning of Mass.

Meanwhile, the boy has gone for the Book, which is at the left of the altar, and he puts it back at the right-hand side, exactly where it was at the beginning of Mass.

The priest goes to it and reads out the prayers which are proper to the day.

The Mass is almost over now. From the middle of the altar, the priest greets the faithful with a *Dominus vobiscum*, and he adds: "Go, the Mass is finished."

But the priest remains at the center of the altar, and all can join in his silent final prayer, his parting words to the Almighty Trinity.

"May the lowly homage of my service be pleasing to Thee, O Most Holy Trinity: and do Thou grant that the Sacrifice, which I, all unworthy, have offered up in the sight of Thy Majesty, may be acceptable to Thee

and, because of Thy loving-kindness, may avail to
atone to Thee for myself, and for all those for whom I
have offered it up. Through Christ Our Lord. Amen."

Then he turns once more to the kneeling crowd and
gives them the answer from the Most High: "May
Almighty God bless you, Father, Son, and Holy Ghost.
Amen." And he blesses them with the Sign of the Cross.

All present solemnly make the Sign of the Cross just as
they did at the beginning of Mass.

But still the priest does not go away, nor the people.
They are all waiting there together to hear yet one more
word that speaks to them of Jesus.

The priest moves to the left of the altar, to the place
where he had read the Gospel before. The Book is there no
longer, but a card stands there, with the beginning of St.
John's Gospel written on it. All the people stand up to listen to the words of this Saint, who knew Jesus for such a
long time, and who loved Him so much:

"In the beginning was the Word, and the Word
   was with God, and the Word was God. . . .
All things were made by Him. . . .
He was the true light which lights every man that
   comes into this world. . . .
The world was made by Him:
and the world knew Him not.
He came to His own, and His own received Him not.
But to those who received Him He gave power to be
   made the sons of God. . . ."

The boy answers: "Thanks be to God"—

Deo Gratias

Made in the USA
Middletown, DE
18 November 2021